Handmade
Embroidered
Bags

Jenny Rolfe

SEARCH PRESS

First published in Great Britain 2005

Search Press Limited
Wellwood, North Farm Road,
Tunbridge Wells, Kent TN2 3DR

Text copyright © Jenny Rolfe 2005

Photographs by Charlotte de la Bédoyère,
Search Press Studios
Photographs and design copyright
© Search Press Ltd 2005

ISBN 1 84448 029 1

The Publishers and author can accept no responsibility
for any consequences arising from the information,
advice or instructions given in this publication.

Readers are permitted to reproduce any of the items/
patterns in this book for their personal use, or for the
purposes of selling for charity, free of charge and
without the prior permission of the Publishers. Any use
of the items/patterns for commercial purposes is not
permitted without the prior permission of the
Publishers.

Suppliers

If you have difficulty in obtaining any of the materials
and equipment mentioned in this book, then please
write to the Publishers, at the address above, for a
current list of stockists. including firms who operate a
mail-order service.

Acknowledgements

*I would like thank The Bramble Patch for
supplying a lot of the fabrics, threads and beads
used in this book, and thanks also to
Oliver Twists for supplying decorative threads.
I would also like to thank European Quilting
Supplies Ltd of Leicester, who supply YLI
threads to shops throughout the UK, for
supplying them to me as well!*

*For helping to proofread my projects, I would
like to thank my friend, Claire Higgott.*

*Special thanks to my daughter Tiffany for her
encouragement and support and to my son,
Ashley, for helping me to understand
my computer.*

*Finally thanks to everyone at Search Press,
particularly Roz Dace and also Sophie and
Juan for making it all come together.*

Publisher's note

All the step-by-step photographs in this book
feature the author, Jenny Rolfe, demonstrating
the making of embroidered bags. No models
have been used.

Contents

Introduction

I have in the past predominantly been a quilter and as such the idea of sitting in front of the fire in the winter, snuggling under a quilt whilst hand stitching it is an appealing one. However, when I had more quilts than beds to put them on, I decided to down-size and started making smaller hangings which increasingly incorporated my second love: embroidery. Then of course I only had so many walls to hang them on, so I had to down-size further!

As bags have been a passion of mine for many years, it seemed a good idea to make my own: you can never have too many bags! I could never find quite what I wanted in the shops. I do find, however, that I still have to go shopping on a regular basis: I tell my husband this is 'research'.

Although these days it is easier to find embroidered bags, there is nothing quite like making your own, as you can put your own unique stamp on them. The bags in this book are all made using free machine embroidery, but do not worry if you have not done this before. I will take you through the basics and show you examples of different stitches and you can let your imagination do the rest.

It is a misconception that you have to have a top of the range sewing machine for free machine embroidery. As long as you can lower the feed dogs or cover them with a plate, you can free machine, however old your sewing machine. It does, of course, take practice, but then so do most things in life. I still sit in front of the fire on a cold winter's night, but now I am adding beads and hand embroidery to my machine embroidered pieces. Go through your stash of fabrics and bits and pieces that you have bought at shows, taken home and then realised you had no idea what to do with: they can be incorporated in your bag designs. The important thing is to enjoy making the bags. I hope you will be inspired by this book and will enjoy making your own unique bags.

Materials

Fabric

A lot of the fabrics used to make these bags can be found at your local quilt or haberdashery shop, such as cottons and silks. You may have to go further afield for different textured fabrics such as metallic organza, chiffon, velvet and netting, although they are becoming more and more available. Half the fun is searching through your stash of bits and pieces that you have bought at quilt and embroidery shows.

A selection of different fabrics

Threads

Machine quilting threads There are many on the market – I like to use the variegated ones. They are usually made from cotton.

Machine embroidery threads Many of these are made from rayon and give a lovely sheen to your surface. They come in many colours.

Metallic threads These are very useful and add texture to your sewing. If you sew quite densely, they catch the light wonderfully.

Invisible thread This is very useful and comes in light and dark. Even threads that are too thick to be used on the top of your sewing machine may be used on the bobbin, and you then sew on the reverse of your fabric, using an invisible thread on the top.

Hand embroidery threads These can be used to enhance your surfaces by couching down, french knots etc. They can also be used to make tassels and covered cords. Crochet threads, perlé, fine ribbons, cords and cotton à broder will all come in handy.

Threads of various types and colours

Sewing machine

A basic sewing machine is all you need – as long as you can either lower the feed dogs or cover the plate, you are ready to go. Keep your machine clean and oiled (if appropriate) at all times – it is amazing how quickly the bobbin area gets clogged up. For the purposes of this book a darning (or open embroidery foot) is essential for free machining. An appliqué foot, which is open at the front so you can see what you are sewing, is not essential but really useful.

Your machine will come with a number of feet. Shown here from left to right are: a basic darning foot for free machining; a similar foot with an open front for free machining; a basic foot for straight stitching and a walking foot which helps to feed the fabric through evenly, making difficult fabrics much easier to sew.

Basic sewing equipment

Scissors You will need a small, sharp, pointed pair for cutting threads and a larger pair for cutting fabrics. Curved scissors are useful but not essential and are used for snipping threads in awkward places. Most importantly keep a pair just for cutting paper and don't let anyone else use your best scissors!

Pins I like to use the flower-headed variety – they are very long and sharp and if I drop any on the floor I can find them easily (very useful when you have animals or small children in the house).

Machine needles I keep a selection of needles – I tend to buy them when I see them in the same way that I buy threads. There are so many needles that you can buy for specific purposes i.e. 'quilting needles', 'metallic needles' and 'denim needles', but I find that top stitch needles are good for most machining purposes including free machining, as they have long eyes and threads don't break as easily. A selection of sizes 80–100 is probably all you will need to start with and as with threads, you can add to them when you see them. The most important thing to remember is that needles can blunt very quickly and need to be replaced frequently – don't wait until they snag your fabric.

Crewel needles For hand stitching, a packet of crewel needles in various sizes should start you off and you can add to these when you need to use very fine or very thick threads.

Curved needles These are useful for sewing rigid edges.

Other useful items include a **seam ripper** for undoing any sewing, a tape measure and thimbles.

Pins; dressmaking, paper and embroidery scissors; seam ripper; tape measure; crewel needles; thimbles; machine needles; sharps and curved needles.

Embellishments

Beads and sequins in all shapes and sizes can be used to embellish your bags. Shisha glass adds a bit of shine and you can make your own by covering washers in threads to match your bag. Hardware shops are interesting places to search around for some of these items and you could also look there for wire in different sizes. Wire can be made into wired covered cords which can then be couched down on to fabric. It can also be threaded with beads and sewn on to a background. Hollow plastic tubing bought from medical suppliers and filled with beads can be used for bag handles, as can plastic bangles or pieces of dowelling.

Beads, sequins, shisha mirrors, wire in various colours, washers and covered washers, all used for embellishing bags.

Hollow plastic tubing, dowelling and bangles for making handles, acrylic paints and a paint brush for painting wooden handles and sequinned ribbon to trim embroidered bags.

Other items

Fusible webbing This is used to bond two fabrics together. It has a non-stick paper backing which can be used for tracing patterns and is ideal for appliqué. Fix using an iron.

Baking parchment (Not greaseproof paper.) This is used to protect your iron.

Fabric glue sticks, fabric adhesive spray, PVA glue and a spatula All useful to keep your pieces of fabric where you want them to be.

Pegs and weights Used to hold parts of bags together while glue dries.

Water soluble film Used on an embroidery frame to create lacy patterns that interlock. When you have finished sewing, you dissolve the film using hot or cold water, and the stitching, once dry, can be sewn on to a background.

Mount board This is very thick card. It can be used as a base for more structured bags and can also be used for winding thread on to make tassels. Always cut it with a craft knife on a cutting mat.

Pencil, eraser and double-sided tape For making templates and designing.

Wire cutters Used to cut wire for embellishing bags.

Ruler This is essential. I like the ones used in conjunction with rotary cutters as they come in a variety of lengths and widths, have grid marks printed on them and are see-through. However, any ruler will do.

Heavyweight interfacing This is used to give shape to more structured bags.

Quilting gloves These are thin gloves that have rubber tips to keep your fabric taut when you are free machine sewing.

Felt This is used as the inside layer of the bags.

String Used for making covered cords (see pages 26–27).

Clockwise from top left: heavyweight interfacing, fusible webbing, baking parchment, iron, spray adhesive, PVA glue, fabric glue stick, spatula, pencil sharpener, eraser, wire cutters, cutting mat, mount board, rotary cutter's ruler, craft knife, water soluble film on an embroidery frame, pens for marking fabric, pencil, pegs, weights, quilting gloves, double-sided tape, felt, string and thin water soluble film.

Design

Three elements are particularly important when you are designing quilted fabric projects like embroidered bags: colour, shape and texture.

For colour, I find that nature is a particularly good source of inspiration: think of spring flowers, summer skies, green fields and leaves as they turn in the autumn.

I like to work with basic shapes such as squares and circles. These are wonderful when repeated or distorted: think of a piece of wire mesh and how you can bend and change it.

Buy a small notebook and every time you see an image that captures your imagination in a magazine or elsewhere, stick it in your notebook. You will soon see a pattern emerging and realize that you are drawn by certain colours and shapes.

Texture is important when it comes to translating your sketches into stitches. This is why I like to work with basic shapes: their simplicity leaves me free to go over the top with texture when stitching and sewing.

When you are out walking, keep an eye out for fallen leaves. They don't need to be perfect – in fact they are more interesting when they have a few holes.

Poppy seed heads are a wonderful shape and texture. I sketched these in pencil and then added a wash with water soluble pencils. Finally I hand stitched a small sample on fabric.

FROM AFRICA - GHANA -
silk Kente cloth -
narrow strip weaving
Late 19th century

INDIA
Wool background -
from Kashmir -
Leaf and cone -
'buta' motifs
from a shawl border

INDIA - Traditional motif of facing parrots.
Worked in chain stitch. Using cotton threads
Centre of shisha glass.

I like to keep samples of old, unusual and foreign textiles for reference. I make notes to remind me of where they came from. The ones on the left and at bottom right are from India and the one on the top right is silk Kente cloth from Ghana.

15

How to start

I love nothing more that getting all my fabrics and threads out at the start of a project. I keep special threads such as machine quilting threads, machine embroidery threads, metallics and rayons in large baskets. I divide them into warm colours: reds, oranges, yellows; neutral colours such as creams, browns, gold, bronze and copper and cool colours like blues, purples and greens. I have other baskets devoted to thicker threads, cords and braids and ribbons in a variety of colours and also beads and sequins and wires.

I keep my cotton fabrics divided into colours and keep special fabrics such as organza, chiffon, velvet, netting and silk together in all different colours.

When I have decided what colour palette I want to use for the new project, I pull out fabrics, threads and beads from every basket and set them out in front of me. This in itself is very inspirational.

These are typical selections from my fabrics and threads, which I have divided into warm, neutral and cool colours.

Here, inspired by the page from my sketchbook shown below, I have chosen threads and fabrics from the 'cool' themed basket, and decorative threads and ribbons to complement them.

I use pencils and water soluble crayons in my sketches to work on the shapes and colour schemes that inspire me.

I then like to make up free machined fabrics in similar colour ways, for instance, all green to all blue, for use in my projects.

I choose threads, beads and embellishments to complete the look.

Techniques

Free machining

This technique might seem complicated at first but once mastered, opens up infinite possibilities. You are in control of the stitching – you can go in any direction, not just forwards. With most machines you need to lower your feed dogs and replace your standard foot with a darning foot. You will need to refer to your sewing machine manual if you need to cover the feed dogs with a plate.

Turn the stitch length and width to 0.

Before embarking on any project you should make sure that your tension is correct. You might need to lower the top tension; do this a little at a time.

Remember that if the bobbin thread comes through to the top, the tension is too tight and if the top thread goes through to the bottom, the tension is too loose.

1. Lower the feed dogs by depressing the button on the side of your machine. Refer to your sewing machine manual if this does not seem to be the method on your machine.

2. Replace your standard foot with the darning foot (or open embroidery foot).

Note

It is a good idea at this time to replace your old needle with a new one – preferably a size 80 Top stitch.

3. Take one piece of fabric and lay it right side down. Place the piece of felt on top and then place the second piece of fabric, right side up on top. Use the spray to keep the fabrics together as 'a quilt sandwich'.

4. Thread the machine embroidery thread on to the machine and on to the bobbin and starting in the middle of the 'quilt sandwich', lower the machine needle into the fabric. Raise the needle and this will bring the bobbin thread up to the surface. Holding the two threads to one side, sew one or two small stitches on top of each other to secure them.

6. Snip off the threads.

5. Wearing quilting gloves, start moving the fabric around to create different shapes.

Free machining patterns

These are all stitches that can be used to fill in a background. It is a good idea to practise these stitches on paper first and once your pencil is flowing on the paper you will be able to do it on fabric as well.

Diagram A

Diagram B

Diagram C

No. 1 This is commonly known as vermicelli or meandering stitch and is the most popular of the filling in stitches.

No. 2 This is a spiral shape. It creates an overall pattern but the same stitch can be used in rows, as can a square version of it (see Diagram A).

No. 3 Circular shapes. These can be boulders or pebbles depending on the size! Good for embroidering paths, beaches etc.

No. 4 Square shapes. Again, you can vary these in size. Large squares cover a surface very quickly. You can elongate the shape and make them into bricks (see Diagram B).

No. 5 This is a wavy line going horizontally and vertically. Very good for filling large spaces very quickly.

No. 6 This particular stitch is very useful for using on skies and water as it flows.

No. 7 This is the vermicelli with an added square every now and then.

No. 8 This is the vermicelli with added twirls and heart shapes. See Diagram C for other vermicelli variations.

Making your own fabric

Making your own background fabric is fun and a variety of effects can be achieved, depending on whether you lay down strips of similar colours or contrasting colours. In this piece I have used different coloured sheer fabrics and a wavy free machine stitch to keep them in place.

You will need

Sewing machine with darning foot

Piece of felt for backing, 20.3cm (8in) square

Piece of fusible webbing, 20.3cm (8in) square

Selection of fabrics: organza, chiffons, lamés, cottons

Baking parchment

Selection of different coloured threads

1. Take your piece of felt backing and lay the fusible webbing on top, paper side up. Press the webbing on to the felt, (refer to the manufacturer's instructions) and leave for a minute before peeling off the paper.

2. Tear strips of your sheer fabrics about 3.8cm (1½in) wide and place them on top of the fusible webbing, overlapping them as you go.

3. When you are happy with the result, carefully place a piece of baking parchment on top and then press lightly to keep them in place.

4. Thread your machine with your chosen thread and lower the feed dogs. Start at one side and wearing quilting gloves, stitch a wavy line up and down the piece, keeping the rows fairly close together. Keep changing your machine thread to match the colour of the background strips.

5. Thread the machine with a contrasting thread and start free machining across and up and down the background, adding circles as you go.

The completed piece of free-machined fabric could be used for any of the bags in this book. You could also try adding thin, torn strips of netting as you free machine and experiment with different quilting stitches.

24

This piece has been more densely free machined and includes beads which were sewn on by hand afterwards. You could sew French knots on to the background to add texture instead of beads.

Making cords

Once you have made your own cords you will never again go out and buy commercial ones as they are great fun to make and will perfectly match your project. You can use fancy threads and an open zigzag stitch so that the threads show through or, if you are covering string, shorten the stitch length to ensure that it is completely covered. When covering string, a useful tip is to use your ordinary threads to cover initially, and then increase the stitch length and do another row in a more decorative thread.

1. Set your sewing machine to the zigzag stitch and fit your appliqué foot. Thread the machine with the same thread on the top and in the bobbin. Take a piece of fine string and place it under the foot, leaving 5cm (2in) behind the foot to hold on to. Set the machine to a zigzag and ensure the stitch is wide enough to cover the string by testing that the needle clears the string on both sides.

2. If the string is not completely covered in the first row, just turn it round and sew over it again.

3. When the string is covered, change your top and bobbin threads to a decorative thread and increase the stitch length. Do one more row to complete the cord.

Note

You can use a cording foot if you have one or lower the feed dogs and use a darning foot. I like the appliqué foot because I can see what I am doing.

Opposite

The finished cord (from bottom left) with a variety of cords in different colours. If you put three cords side by side, you can sew them together with a zigzag stitch to make a wider cord or plait them together to make a chunkier cord.

Petal Bag

This tasselled little bag is very easily made from two folded circles and a lot of free machining. It reminds me of a flower gradually opening up and the petals unfurling.

You will need

Sewing machine with darning foot

Quarter metre (10in) fabric for the outside of the bag

Quarter metre (10in) felt

Quarter metre (10in) lining fabric

Plate 16.5cm (6 ½in) in diameter

Fabric adhesive spray

Twelve lengths of a variety of textured and decorative threads 127cm (50in) long for the handle and five lengths 150cm (60in) long for the tassel

Tiny beads

Two small washers

Machine quilting thread

Small piece of mounting card, cutting mat and craft knife

PVA glue and spatula

Fine marker

Scissors and pins

1. Take your main piece of fabric and cut out a piece 17.7 x 35.5cm (7 x 14in). On the right side draw two circles with a fine marker, using the plate as a template.

Note

A quarter metre (10in) assumes that the fabric or felt is 112cm (44in) wide, so that your piece will measure 25 x 112cm (10 x 44in).

2. Take the piece of felt and cut out a piece 17.7 x 35.5cm (7 x 14in). Spray with the fabric adhesive spray. Place the fabric on top.

3. Thread the machine with machine quilting thread, lower the feed dogs and attach the darning foot. Fill the marked shapes with free machine circles. When complete, sew round the edge on the drawn line.

4. Carefully cut out the circles just outside the sewn line and sew tiny beads at random all over their surface.

5. Take your lining fabric and cut out a piece 17.7 x 35.5cm (7 x 14in). Draw round the plate twice and cut out the circles. Place your machined and beaded circles right side down and spray the backs with glue. Position the lining circles on top. They may be slightly larger as the fabric shrinks when quilted, so you may need to trim a small amount of lining from the edge of each circle.

6. Put the machine back to normal sewing and attach an appliqué foot. Set the stitch to zigzag and sew round the edge of each lined circle. You might have to do this twice to cover the edges.

7. Fold the circular petals in half to get the shape of the bag and secure with pins.

8. Put tiny dabs of PVA glue on the underside of each petal and place a heavy book on top of the bag until the glue dries.

9. Take the twelve decorative, textured threads 127 cm (50 in) long. Divide them into three groups of four. Take one group and cover it with zigzag stitch, as when making a cord. Make the zigzag stitch very wide and the stitch length very long so that the threads show through. Repeat with the other groups of thread to make three cords.

10. Anchor the three zigzagged cords; here they are pinned to a basket. Plait them together.

11. Feed the plaited threads through a washer for about 2.5cm (1in) and fold back the end.

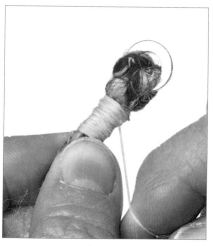

12. Thread a needle with a matching thread and wrap the loose ends. Repeat the other end.

13. Using the same thread, sew the washers by hand on to each side of the bag.

14. To make the tassel, cut a piece of mounting card, 11.5 x 5cm (4½ x 2in). Take your five threads, hold them at the bottom of the card and wrap them round several times.

15. Thread a needle with a long length of the same thread as you used in step 12 and tie at the top.

16. Cut the threads at the bottom of the card.

17. Taking the threaded needle, wrap the yellow thread round the top of the tassel where you tied it. Then take the needle up through the top of the tassel.

18. Using the same yellow thread, bind round the collar of the tassel.

19. To tie off, push the needle back down through the tassel and cut the thread.

20. Use dressmaking scissors to trim the bottom of the tassel.

21. Sew the tassel on to the bottom of the bag using the same yellow thread.

The finished Petal Bag

35

In this version, decorative threads have been knotted at intervals for the handle.

French knots could be added instead of beads and smaller versions of the bag could be made by varying the size of the original circle.

Mezzaluna Bag

I had the idea for this bag when I was chopping herbs one day. I was using a mezzaluna, which is a piece of kitchen equipment with a curved blade and a handle on each side. Mezzaluna means 'half moon' in Italian.

You will need

Sewing machine with a darning foot and an appliqué or cording foot

Quarter metre (10in) of three different coloured cotton fabrics

Quarter metre (10in) of felt

Quarter metre (10in) of fusible webbing

Various threads to match

Decorative threads for couching

Invisible thread

Length of tubing, 30.5cm (12in)

Beads small enough to thread through the tubing

Length of wire, 40.5cm (16in), thin enough to thread the beads on to

Tiny beads

Fabric glue stick

Fabric adhesive spray

Baking parchment and iron

Quilting gloves

Fine marker

Large needle

Pins

Note

A quarter metre (10in) assumes that the fabric or felt is 112cm (44in) wide, so that your piece will measure 25 x 112cm (10 x 44in).

Patterns for the front and back and for the base of the bag, printed half size. Enlarge them to double the size on a photocopier, trace them, stick the tracings on to thicker paper and cut the templates out. Mark the position of the dots.

1. Cut a piece of felt and a piece of fusible webbing, each 20.3 x 47cm (8 x 18½in). Press the webbing on to the felt and peel off the backing paper. Tear the three different colours of cotton fabric into strips about 4cm (1½in) wide. Cut the strips into 20.3cm (8in) lengths and place them on top of the fusible webbing, overlapping slightly so that the background does not show.

2. Place a piece of baking parchment on top and press with an iron.

3. Set up your machine with thread suitable for machine quilting; I have used a variegated thread here. Lower the feed dogs and attach your darning foot. Wearing your quilting gloves, sew a large vermicelli pattern all over the surface.

39

4. Sew across the strips of fabric with a wavy stitch, keeping the lines of stitching quite close together.

5. Take your decorative threads and couch them on to the background. Use an invisible thread on top and an ordinary thread in the bobbin. Set your machine to zigzag wide enough to cover the threads that you are couching.

Note

To couch threads you can either use an appliqué foot or a cording foot. The cording foot has a groove underneath it that lets thicker threads go through more easily. I prefer to use an appliqué foot as I can see what I am doing.

6. Choose one of the fabrics for the base and cut a piece approximately 10 x 28cm (4 x 11in). Also cut a piece of felt the same size. Using the fabric adhesive spray, bond the fabric and felt. To quilt the base, put a thicker thread on the bobbin and an invisible thread on the top of the machine. Lower the feed dogs and attach the darning foot. Place the base of the bag felt side up under the needle and free machine circles over the entire surface.

7. When you turn the base over, the thicker thread will appear on the right side.

Note

This method works well with any thread that does not sew easily when threaded on the top, such as thick threads and some metallic threads.

8. For the lining, choose one of your fabrics and draw and cut out a front, back and base using the templates and a fine marker.

9. With right sides together, pin the lining base to the lining front, matching the dots. Change your machine to normal sewing and sew between the dots, removing pins as you go. Do the same with the lining back.

10. Sew the side seams of the lining from the dots to the top edge.

11. Position the front and back templates on the reverse of the couched fabric as in the diagram below. Position the base template on the reverse of the quilted base fabric. Draw around the templates with a fine marker, marking the dots as before.

12. Sew along all the drawn lines to ensure that the couching and stitching does not unravel. Cut out just outside the line. Keep the remnants of the couched fabric – they will be used later.

13. Stitch the base to the front and back in the same way as you did with the lining.

43

14. Turn the bag right side out. Place the lining in the bag and tack around the top edge. Thread up your machine with a matching thread on the top and in the bobbin and change to a zigzag stitch. Sew around the top edge until covered.

15. To make the handle, thread the wire through the tubing and bend it over at one end to ensure the beads stay in place. Start threading your beads on to the other end of the wire until you have filled the whole tube. Bend the wire over at the other end.

16. To attach the handle to the bag, take a large needle and make a hole at the top of the side seam. Remove the needle and thread one end of the wire through the hole. Bend upwards and wind round the base of the tubing. Make a corresponding hole on the other side of the bag, unravel the other end of the wire and secure in the same way.

17. Sew tiny beads down each side, around the base and around the top of the bag.

The finished Mezzaluna Bag. To make the tag, draw a heart shape on the remnants of the bag fabric. Sew a line round the drawn line and cut out the shape just outside this line. Repeat to make another heart. Take a thick thread or cord about 20.3cm (8in) long and wrap it with two rows of zigzags. Place the hearts wrong sides together. Fold the cord and place the ends in between the top of the hearts. Secure with a little fabric glue. Sew round the edge of the hearts with a zigzag stitch.

The size of the bag could be altered by enlarging or reducing the pattern. You can also make tags in different shapes.

Boxy Bag

I used to love my grandmother's knitting bag which had wooden handles, and thought I would make an updated version, although rather smaller.

The pattern for the spiral, shown full size. Transfer it on to card and cut it out to make a template.

You will need

Sewing machine with darning foot and appliqué foot

Quarter metre (10in) of light fabric

Quarter metre (10in) of dark fabric

Quarter metre (10in) of fusible webbing

Quarter metre (10in) of felt

25cm (10in) heavyweight interfacing

Threads to match fabrics

¾ metre (30in) ribbon

Fabric glue stick

Invisible thread

Two pieces of dowelling, each 23cm (9in) long

Acrylic paint and brush

PVA glue

Iron

Needle

Scissors

Pins and pegs

Note

A quarter metre (10in) assumes that the fabric or felt is 112cm (44in) wide, so that your piece will measure 25 x 112cm (10 x 44in).

1. Cut six strips, 15.2 x 5cm (6 x 2in) in the dark fabric and six strips in the light fabric. For the front, lay five strips side by side, alternating the colours. Make an identical set for the back. The remaining two pieces will be the sides. For the base of the bag cut one piece 19 x 5cm (7½ x 2in).

2. Sew the five strips for the bag front together with a 6mm (¼in) seam allowance and press the seams open.

3. Cut 6mm (¼in) off each side so that each piece measures 19 x 15.2cm (7½ x 6in).

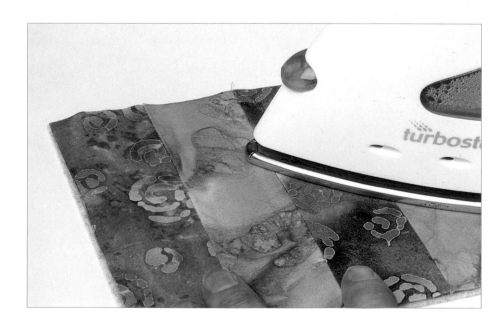

4. Take the felt and the fusible webbing and out of each of these cut two pieces 19 x 15.2cm (7½ x 6in), two pieces 15.2 x 5cm (6 x 2in) and one piece 19 x 5cm (7½ x 2in). Place the fusible webbing on to the back of the bag front and press. Peel off the backing and then press on to the piece of felt. Do this also to the bag back, the two sides and the base.

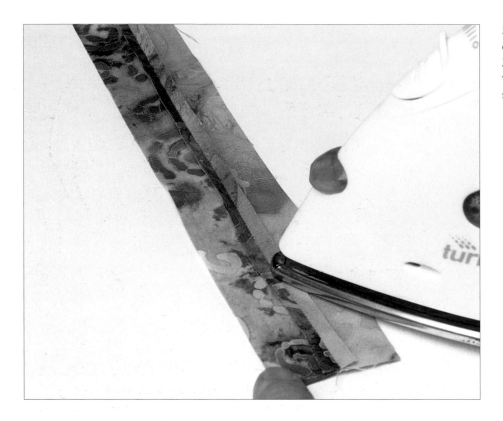

5. Cut two strips of fabric, one in dark, the other in light, 2.5 x 30.5cm (1 x 12in). Sew these together and press the seam open.

6. Cut a piece of fusible webbing 3.8 x 30.5cm (1½ x 12in) and press it on to the back of the strip. Take the spiral template and use a fine marker to draw around it eight times along the length of the strip. Cut out the shapes and peel off the backing.

7. Place four spirals on the front of the bag and four on the back, positioning them so that the colours reverse and the seam lines line up with the seam lines on the bag. Press.

50

8. Cut a 3.8 x 25cm (1½ x 10in) strip of dark fabric and a piece of fusible webbing the same size and bond them together. Using the same spiral template, cut out seven spirals and bond two on each of the side pieces and three on the base.

9. Set your machine to a zigzag stitch and using invisible thread, sew round the outside of these shapes with a small open stitch. Do this on the front, the back, both sides and the base.

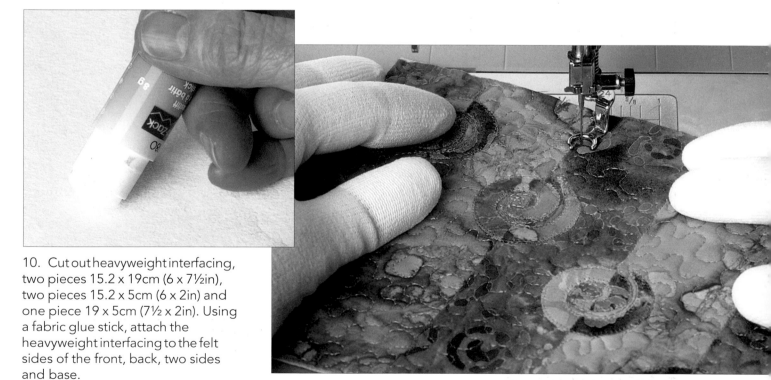

10. Cut out heavyweight interfacing, two pieces 15.2 x 19cm (6 x 7½in), two pieces 15.2 x 5cm (6 x 2in) and one piece 19 x 5cm (7½ x 2in). Using a fabric glue stick, attach the heavyweight interfacing to the felt sides of the front, back, two sides and base.

11. Lower the feed dogs on your machine and attach a darning foot. Using threads to match your fabrics, free machine a vermicelli stitch over the surfaces of all five pieces. Trim the edges if necessary.

12. For the lining, take one of your fabrics and cut two pieces 15.2 x 19cm (6 x 7½in), two pieces 15.2 x 5cm (6 x 2in) and one piece 19 x 5cm (7½ x 2in). Use the fabric glue stick on the back of the heavyweight interfacing and stick it on to the lining pieces.

13. Change your machine back to normal stitching and attach the appliqué foot. Set to a medium width zigzag stitch and sew round the edges of all pieces with a matching thread. Depending on how closely you stitch, you might have to go round the edges once or twice to cover.

14. For the tags, cut four pieces of heavyweight interfacing, 3.2 x 11.5cm (1¼ x 4½in) and four pieces of the dark fabric 3 x 13.3cm (3½ x 5¼). Fold the fabric over the interfacing as shown, apply fabric glue stick to keep it in place, and press it. Change your machine back to free machining and sew a vermicelli stitch all over the tags.

15. Place the tag in line with the first seam, leaving the zigzagged edge clear, and secure it with a pin. Fold the tag down to the inside of the bag to form a loop. Using thread to match the tag, secure the tag firmly to the bag. Repeat with the other tags, placing one in each corner of the bag, front and back.

16. Use ladder stitch and invisible thread to hand stitch the two sides of the bag and the base together.

17. Sew this strip to the front of the bag and then sew it to the back.

18. Take your lengths of dowelling, paint them with acrylic paint and allow them to dry. Put a little PVA glue inside the top of each tag and slip the dowelling inside. Put a peg on each side of each tag to keep the dowelling handles secure and leave for an hour to dry.

19. Attach the ribbon to the top of the bag with tiny dabs of PVA glue.

The finished Boxy Bag

Appliqué was added to these bags, together with beads and ribbon.

This bag has a checkerboard pattern and covered washers over shisha mirrors.

57

Bangles Bag

This bag was inspired by a shop selling an abundance of pretty accessories including brightly coloured plastic bangles in various different shapes. The bangles seemed ideal for use as handles, and could be chosen to complement the fabric and threads used, as well as the shape of the bag.

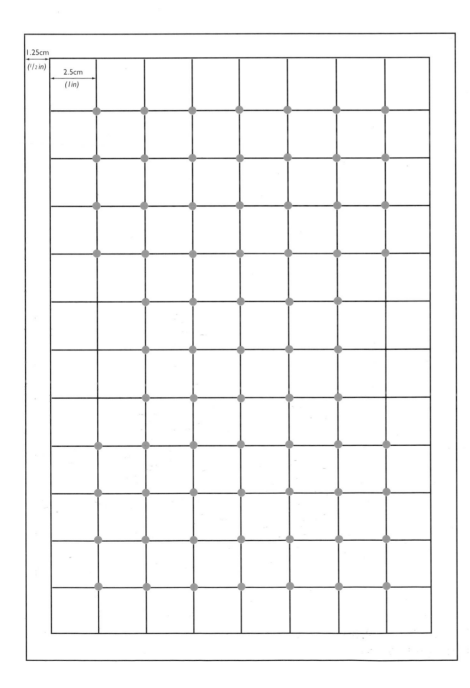

1.25cm
(¹/₂in)

2.5cm
(1in)

You will need

Quarter metre (10in) of main fabric
Quarter metre (10in) of felt
Quarter metre (10in) of lining fabric
Variety of metallic threads
Beads
Two bangles
Mounting card, craft knife and cutting mat
Rotary cutter's or ordinary ruler
PVA glue and spatula
Fabric adhesive spray
Fabric glue stick
Small piece of heavyweight interfacing
Pins
Weights
Needle
Iron

Note

A quarter metre (10in) assumes that the fabric or felt is 112cm (44in) wide, so that your piece will measure 25 x 112cm (10 x 44in).

The pattern for the grid, printed half size. The pattern also shows where the beads should go.

1. Take your main fabric and cut out a piece 33 x 23cm (13 x 9in). Using a fine marker, draw the grid lines on the fabric as shown on the pattern opposite. I find that using a rotary cutting ruler like the one shown is helpful as it has a grid printed on it and you can see through it, but you could use an ordinary ruler.

2. Take your felt and cut out a piece 33 x 23cm (13 x 9in). Spray with the fabric adhesive spray and place your fabric on top, grid side up.

3. Set your machine to normal sewing and if you have one, attach a walking foot. Sew along all the grid lines with a metallic thread on top and a normal sewing thread in a matching colour underneath.

4. Lower the feed dogs, attach the darning foot and start sewing up and down in alternate squares. This can be a continuous process, working diagonally across the grid as shown in the diagram on the left.

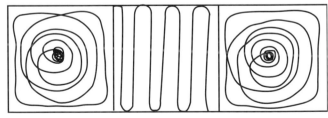

5. In the remaining squares, start in the middle and sew in a spiral towards the edge, then come back in again and finish off with two or three stitches in the middle, as shown in the diagram on the right.

6. Sew on the beads as shown in the pattern on page 58, leaving spaces for sewing up the bag.

7. Fold the bag right sides together and pin along the edges, aligning the grid lines. Sew along each side and trim the edges down to 6mm (¼in).

8. Fold back the bottom corner edge and measure 5cm (2in). You will be able to see on the reverse where your stitching is. Pin and then stitch across. Do the same to the other corner edge.

9. Carefully turn the bag right sides out to make sure you have sewn evenly and then press the seams open. Sew the remaining beads along the two edges and at the bottom. Leave the top until later.

10. Use a craft knife, cutting mat and ruler to cut a piece of mounting card to 15.2 x 5cm (6 x 2in).

11. Put dabs of glue on the base of the bag and put the mounting card on top. Place weights in the bag and leave for an hour.

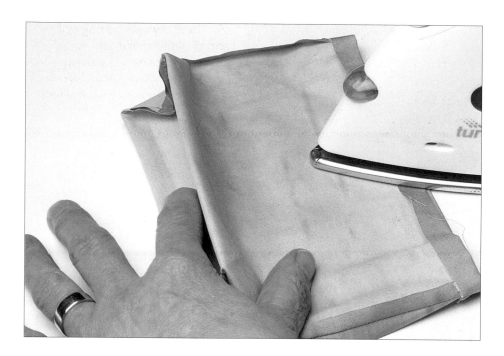

12. Sew the lining in the same way as the bag including the corner edges. Cut off the excess and press the seams open. Fold over the top edge 1.3cm (½in) and press.

13. Place the lining inside the bag. Fold over the 1.3cm (½in) seam allowance at the top of the bag and pin the lining and bag together.

14. For the tags holding down the bangles, cut two pieces of heavyweight inferfacing 1.3 x 10cm (½ x 4in) and two pieces of the main fabric 4.4 x 10cm (1¾ x 4in). Place the interfacing on top of the fabric. Apply fabric glue stick to the interfacing and fold over. Press with an iron.

15. With metallic thread, sew up and down the tags and then fold them over each of the bangles and insert the ends in the centre of each side as close as possible to the bag. Tack all the way round.

16. Using metallic thread, sew as close to the top of the bag as possible to secure it.

17. Sew beads along the top row of the bag to finish it.

The basic shape for this bag can be varied to make it wider or taller. It can be made with fabric you have made yourself or with crazy patchwork.

66

Crazy Patchwork Bag

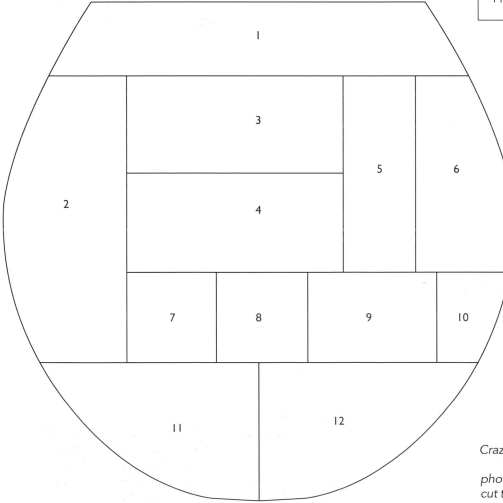

The lovely thing about crazy patchwork is that you can use different weights of fabric as they are laid onto a background piece and then sewn down. It is a nice idea to take pieces of fabric or beads that mean something to you, such as fabric left over from making a child's dress or buttons and beads from your mother's button box, and incorporate these into the finished item. This particular bag was inspired by a beautiful bouquet of flowers I was given, all purples and greens.

You will need

Selection of fabrics: silk, lamé, velvet, cotton

Threads to match

Fusible webbing, 23 x 40.7cm (9 x 16in)

Felt, 23 x 40.7cm (9 x 16in)

Baking parchment and iron

Beads

Four 1.5cm (⅝in) washers

Double-sided tape and PVA glue

43cm (17in) length of medium gauge wire and larger beads for the handle

Various variegated and metallic threads for machine embroidery

25.4cm (10in) square piece of water soluble film and a 17.8cm (7in) embroidery hoop

Pins

The pattern for the Crazy Patchwork Bag, shown at 75 per cent of full size. Enlarge it on a photocopier, transfer it on to card and cut the shape out to make a template.

68

1. Use the template to cut out two pieces of fusible webbing. Place them on top of the felt and press with an iron. Cut round the shapes and peel off the backing paper.

2. Transfer the full size pattern on to thin paper and number each piece. Cut out the pieces.

3. Take the paper pieces and pin them on to your chosen fabrics. Cut round each piece twice, making one set for the front and one set for the back.

5. Place on an ironing board and put a piece of baking parchment on top. Press very gently without moving the iron backwards and forwards to prevent the pieces from moving.

4. Lay each piece of fabric on your background felt, fusible webbing right side up, following the numbering. Make sure no background is showing.

6. Set up the sewing machine for normal sewing. Use a variegated thread and do a trial piece: choose three or four of the standard stitches on your sewing machine, suitable for covering the raw edges. You can use just a satin stitch if you wish. Start to sew along the joins between fabric pieces, beginning with the line between pieces 3 and 4. Then sew all the vertical lines, and finish off by sewing the horizontal lines.

7. Now is your chance to embellish the background fabric pieces. Do some free machining in different patterns. To make the star pattern, start in the middle and sew round and round to make a circle. Then take the needle up as if to twelve o'clock and add a little circle. Sew back down to the bottom of the central circle, then sew down to six o'clock and add another little circle. Repeat at three o'clock and nine o'clock. Now fill in all the other points on the clock in the same way, so that you have a twelve-pointed star.

8. Add beads, but do not sew them too close to the edge seam allowance. Repeat steps 4 to 8 to make the back of the bag.

71

9. To make your own shisha mirrors, attach a small amount of double-sided tape to the back of a washer and peel off the backing. This will secure the thread as you start wrapping.

10. Cut lengths of three different threads, thread them all through a needle and knot the ends together. Tie on to the washer, on top of the sticky tape, and wrap the thread round and round the washer until it is covered. Secure the end.

11. Place the covered washer on top of a piece of shisha glass or a large sequin and secure with PVA glue. Then glue it on to your background fabric and put it aside until it is completely dry.

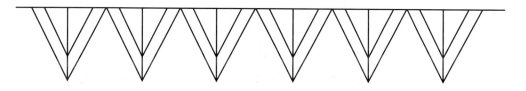

The pattern for the lacy border, shown full size.

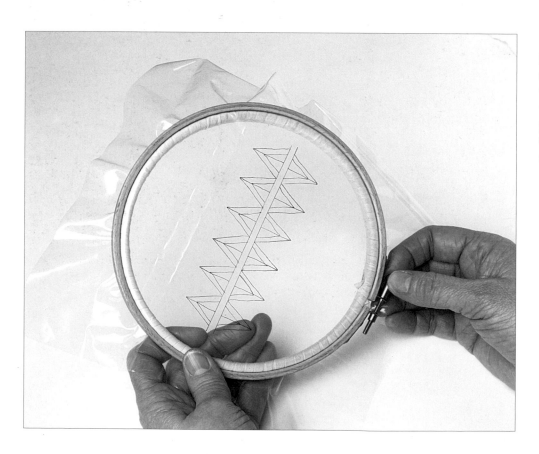

12. To make your lacy border, take your water soluble film and trace off the pattern shown above twice, as shown in the photograph. Secure the water soluble film in your embroidery hoop.

13. Set your sewing machine to free machining, lower the feed dogs and attach the darning foot. With metallic thread on top and in the bobbin, sew over the pattern, linking up all the stitches in each border. Follow the manufacturer's instructions to dissolve the water soluble film and allow the two borders to dry. Sew a bead on to the bottom of each triangle as shown.

14. Place a lacy border 3mm (⅛in) from the top of the bag. Set the machine for normal sewing and secure the top of the border with a straight stitch. Repeat with the other border on the back of the bag.

15. Take one of your fabrics and cut a 3.2 x 45.7cm (1¼ x 18in) strip. Pin it, right sides together round the edges of the front piece.

16. Change to normal thread and sew round with a 6mm (¼in) seam allowance. Attach the back piece in the same way so that the strip forms a gusset. Turn the bag right sides out.

17. Using the original template, cut out front and back pieces of lining and a 3.2 x 45.7cm (1¼ x 18in) strip for a gusset. Sew them together in the same way as the bag.

18. Place the lining inside the bag and pin it round the top. Sew a row of straight stitches round the top, then trim.

19. Change the machine to zigzag stitch and with metallic thread on the top and in the bobbin, sew round the top to neaten the edge.

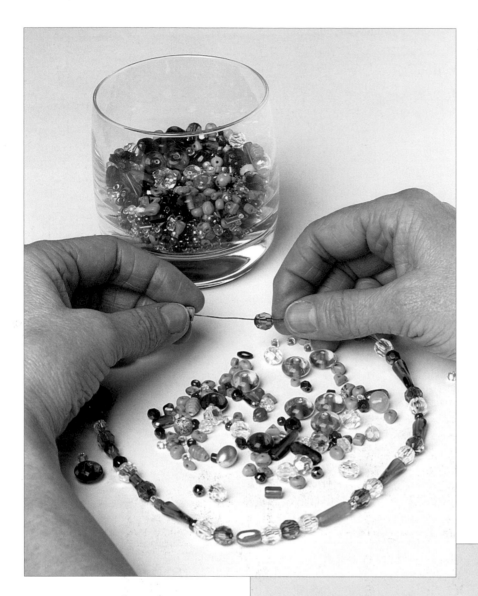

20. Take your piece of wire and thread it with the beads.

21. Attach the beaded wire handle by making a hole in the side of the bag with a large needle, and then threading the wire through the hole and wrapping round to finish off. Do the same to the other side.

The finished Crazy Patchwork Bag

You could make your own crazy patterns or use different shaped pieces to bond to the background. You could also cover the seams by sewing ribbons over them or couching thicker threads.

79

Index